An astonishing precision of language pervades these twenty-one portraits of a mind's intercourse with the world. . . . In the final essay, an homage to San Francisco, he writes that the city's "small particulars" are "cherished here as amplitude . . . as immensity." Cherishing the complex specificities of language and experience is clearly Shurin's ambition and creed. In *King of Shadows*, he brilliantly succeeds.

— Robert Marshall, *Lambda Book Report*

In these 21 essays [*King of Shadows*] — an intimate charting to more than four gay decades — Shurin reveals a multitude of selves: the young student diving with sensual pleasure into sexual San Francisco; . . . the "lovechild of Denise Levertov and Robert Duncan," dedicating his soul to the purity of poetry. . . . One by one, these resonant fragments — drawn from everyday life with a poet's delicate touch — coalesce into a vibrant mini-autobiography.

— Richard Labonte, *Book Marks* (Top Ten)

The Paradise of Forms is about ravishment and the interminable sweet music box of the heart. . . . Among the temptations and the continuous thunder of bodies, Shurin carves out a poetics of male subjectivity that is infinitely complex, prodigal, and sublime. . . . [He] has cut a path which not only links him to the likes of Robert Duncan, John Wieners, and Jack Spicer . . . but lets him claim a prominent place in contemporary American letters.

— Chris Tysh, *Poetry Flash*

Citizen

Citizen

AARON SHURIN

City Lights Books • San Francisco

Cover art, "The Old House," by Su Blackwell / www.sublackwell.co.uk

Thanks to the editors of the following publications and websites, where some of these poems first appeared:
Are You Outside the Lines, Clamor, Denver Quarterly, Eleven Eleven, New American Writing, Omnidawn Publishing, PIP/Project for Innovative Poetry, Rumpus, Sentence, Switchback, Zyzzyva.

Special thanks to the San Francisco Museum of Modern Art for the symposium, "Joinery: Poems on the Occasion of Martin Puryear," which became the genesis for this book, and to the University of San Francisco for a sabbatical that deeply fostered the work.

Library of Congress Cataloging-in-Publication Data
Shurin, Aaron, 1947–
Citizen / Aaron Shurin.
      p. cm.
ISBN 978-0-87286-520-4
I. Title.
PS3569.H86C58 2011
811'.54—dc23

                              2011033565

City Lights Books are published at the City Lights Bookstore, 261 Columbus Avenue, San Francisco, CA 94133.
Visit our website: www.citylights.com

CONTENTS

I: *Flare*

II: *Gather*

III: *Hive*

I.

Flare

COOL DUST

A heave of afternoon light pulls a tulip from the turf, a bower for locusts, a cup of shells. The farmhouse tilts, a bent shadow on wheels. In cedar rooms a family is molded, silent, wrapped in the wire of steel eyes and stopped voice, romantic ash. This is not my house, my ghost, my uninvited guest, my lost labor of love, my thicket or grease, my JPEG gessoed or rawhide suit. The yellow light throbs like an internal organ — soft body of an overture to insect sounds — sapling of a new world — whose future awaits me at the tilting window of my own domestic hut. Perhaps this *is* my mesh of hours, my muscular ache, my guardian sash, twist of rope carved around an old maple trunk, my rod of power red with anticipatory friction at the edge of an emerging set of planetary rings. Stained ochre by the air I pitch forward, a vanilla-scented pear that floats or falls. In the rattan chair on the front porch by the blistered boards of the front door a figure of tar watches. Cool dust sparkles and settles. Shadows have made me visible. An empty wagon flares on the hillside.

CHALICE

Found a trophy in the distant dumb luck — me, the
dowager of chance! A sheep in self's clothing, I threw a
cone of silence over my desk and parceled out the hash:
dream timber, tales of subsistence, true-believer cloth-
ing. I filled the groaning catapult and fired to horizon, a
big pairing of *what* and *whatever*. In a rain of particulars
walls settled against windows — sanctuary fence posts
— reliquary doorjambs — and me slouched in the arm-
chair reading with the radio on. The back stairs turn
toward the attic in a flush of oak; something pulled the
hidden lever on my cross and made a wheel. Lazily I
stroke my stash. Supine giant, somnolent nest: I bury
my face in your smoldering lap . . . my smoldering face
in your lap . . .

STEEPED

A room of thought is wedged between *the androgyny of hair* and *new leaves gasping for light*. Membrane of membrane, skin of my crown. I thought a forest bound by kinship towers — elusive in the blue glow inside the gray cloudbank — indigo friction — a hurricane cult — where his eyes boring over my shoulders fall like hot breath, gravity failing. He is whirling like a haystack, engineered in twilight, his syllables aquatic, lullaby stutter. Scale of my scale, raveling hive. A skateboarder rocks the concrete, cutting the muscle of silence. You, too, seeping memories, as we spin in place. An epiphyte: a love nest. Inextricable, shadow for shadow, rhyme for rhyme.

POSITIONED

A thought without a body is not a star. The yellow house in spring behind the yellow leaves, as if the sun *meant* to land there, squeezed between gray walls like a trap-door, an exit sign . . . And so positioned as if the day itself had escaped the cartographer's lock she polished her eyes beside the windows — always windows and doors — and generated fractions — phrases, we call them — rain-filled hoof-prints and mica strands — refracted in the looming glass like a sphere shedding horizons. Who was her secret polar tug, her bell pull, her Adam cup? Was she raising or lowering ladders inside the staggered light, head down as if in thought but seeing the mounted sky; the peeling, corrugated bark; the coppery cigarette butts and polished plywood table tops and dripping mugs of ale, lit up like sunset gulls bound on the dive . . . ? Did she shiver in the shower of filaments themselves shivering, flared up in the corners and planes where they fell and streamed for her mouth and ears? The body of my star is a thought she plucks from the air that calls her name . . . astronomer . . . wholly intemperate . . . the chandelier of noon . . . her cheekbone perched on her index finger while the patterns spread . . . vibrating frame . . . giant wingèd brain . . . imminence . . .

SPRING BREEZE

I'm as stupid as a spitball in a jumpsuit. Look at my
catalogue of terrors — the marquee says, Inclined To-
ward Medieval Defenses — who gave chase, while the
morning thrummed, to a pillage of pigeons on the bal-
cony — whoopee, a nosedive! — but kept the midnight
searchlights on. Citywide, librarians mark you "over-
due," brought to abandon by the fall of your syllables
after the rise, narcoleptic euphony. But is it you or I at
stake in this topical heat, and whose shady purposes ex-
humed us, plated wet and uninhibited like dinner eels?
The sentence with its unshakeable sentence — captive
logic — as the two-tone synergy churns; the beautiful
sentence, marsupial: conjugal folds. A man crosses his
arms in a liquid maneuver, intractable but pliant, his
feet already planted in second position; the marquee
says, At Home In The Spiral Prospectus. Or your face
in the searchlight projected, sincere and unembellished:
a charismatic stupor that equals the sky . . .

THE DENSITY

Descending the day with no *escalier*, though the heat could squeeze you through — *I thought a being more than vast* — as if the flutters at the edge of sight — as if the downpour in the distance — as if the moister scroll unfurled *behind* the curtain . . . Then a luna moth in the paradigm air flew right to a eucalyptus tree on green dust — congruity of mint and menthol — where the coiled air, almost verbal, whisked a wind of powder into a sheath, cool like an emerald, pilfered like an emerald, inward like an emerald . . . Through what convergence of root and sap did he find himself inside this swollen air? Who was his ally among the overgrown paths — transitory migrations — as the flaps sealed and the columns telescoped and the insects whirred and the buses squealed and his buttons popped and the storefronts flew open while the pine cones burst in the coloratura heat on scales of exhaustion and release? Nothing was his alone, limited to him alone. He perched on a low rock wall in the trumpeting air and licked a globe of sweat from the groove of his lip. More gathered there.

ARTESIAN

A drop of saliva awakens the ink stain. Fumbling at the
doorknob in the ponderous rain . . . repeating in Spanish
the phrases that say you'll be early or late, tall or thin,
naked or clothed, rough like a buzz saw or rolled in
dandelions. Now the notebooks soaked with anticipa-
tion release their codes — accidental courtship — shud-
dering on the threshold of a sealed envelope, steamed to
satisfaction — knuckles like nipples, swollen with mem-
ory and dangerously alert in exile. How he sits polishing
loaves of bread with a dishcloth, grumbling about the
efficacy of yeast while the new dough bubbles and spits.
A vast collection of seminary juices, a terminus of road-
side friction . . . spun sugar . . . cortical vortex . . . your
halo a golden hole . . . germinal discus . . . impossible,
inevitable, incoming . . .

THE TIPPING POINT

From love one takes cargo to reeds right through the vanishing point behind the weathered trees . . . Behind the weathered trees where the rusty water runs — archaic grooves — like a carriage in a 19ᵗʰ century novel with its shutters drawn but its door unlatched and a hand waving frantically go or stay, go *and* stay . . . Swifts burst into wheeling formation — evangelists of the updraft — as we stomp down the hay to convey our *déjeuner,* laid out on the buckaroo blanket limp as catkins. Slowly exhale; the seminar of his ribs. For something love I would split the pit of that something person open, and spit the seeds down a path of perspective lengthening in the shadows. Tenderness *swells*; the wolf-teeth *retract*; a nimbus *descends*; the glottal stop *sings*; a totem *commands*; a totem *revives*; a totem *conceives* . . .

CONVECTION

For a day parsed into segments — woke at Yellow Aw-
ning, worked, ate lunch together through Medallion
Aisles, worked hard, had a scotch or mescal at Diam-
eter, studied, had a light dinner during Honeycomb,
studied more or watched TV or read till we tucked our-
selves into bed at Smoky Tendrils, or sometimes stayed
up talking late into Slipping Staircase till we fell im-
mobilized onto the blankets, glazed like burnt sugar . . .
That story we are toting in our pockets and gums, our
rolled-up trouser legs and bouncy shoes, in our ageing
elbow and knee creases — red-faced finches and rising
incense and an artifactual pulpit of carved copal with its
salamander glyphs and distant spent volcano — as we
shuck our greasy uniforms, stained from cochineal and
chili paste . . . wavered at the apex of the hour in the
liquored heat . . . we sweep the floor where the water
jug broke and scrutinize the blinking shards . . . elabo-
rated affinities . . . dust smell and gas fumes of the aged
city by uneven foot down the close streets with syrupy
air under great flowering clouds in the thick of bodies
crammed into an afternoon swell on the heaving val-
ley floor through visionary traffic snarls over rounded
stones . . . thunderstorms there at the scrim of the hill

every day advancing . . . our faces drenched as we rush
for cover . . . crafted genealogies . . . our thunderstruck,
silent, upturned faces drenched . . .

TRACINGS

Ringtones, steam whistles, church bells — those waxing moons — low hum of the refrigerator, my co-conspirator . . . Meaty brain and its hot comet trails . . . She traces relations in polished black pottery — her seed casings — set up in rows of continuous phrases . . . insignia twine . . . At noon he opens his waterfall smile (swoop down on me right there) as I fumble to unwrap my restless hair from its old, tight weave — *danza de la pluma* — in the old city's new space, a wriggling nest of husbands and brides . . . Who I have sought or asked; who have sought me and asked me . . . every morning . . . Griddled in scallion oil so that the pods open and the custard blooms . . . Traveler crouched on the corner *mouthing the stone* foundations: gastronomer . . . Hot plaza wavers, closes in like a scorched flower . . . And the wild, encircling clouds . . . the charging clouds . . . the century of clouds . . .

WITHOUT BORDERS

Would've brought my tablet to the table in the sun-
beam; could've taken the tongs and placed each name
in a matchbox for safekeeping; might've swirled my
tongue inside the shell forever, alluvial redemption . . .
Kettle for boiling berries and making ink, but we *haven't*
gone post-apocalyptic — loped through the house
swirling his grin with a sign that read "Resistance is Fu-
tile" — mounds up the pillows and burrows his face for
the pure symmetry of sleep. Then the students — those
cauldrons — are splashing his sheeted head with a tonic
of lime buds and guava — "Teacher, teacher: teach!"
— stretch . . . *and feed on prime* . . . Purely local throng,
escalating tingle . . . Vented neighborhood . . . Scouring
the bare, polished room for information, seams split . . .
Resistance is fertile . . .

THROTTLE BOY

As if melted in the sun, dispersed by the fog, taken
apart by the mountain wind, shriveled in the rain, and
left standing unencumbered in a pearly glow of emp-
ty velocity — that's a *good* thing, mate — shedding
quadrant and armband, pointed hat and rolled scroll
— salute the ground *above* you — at the center of a
vector-ball he gasps for coordinates but tries to sustain
contradiction, flashing like a tin mirror at noon . . .
And for all that he'd like to be comprehensively frisked
inside the reeling plaza and its greenstone dusk —
always scamp eyes — he honors the rising bulbous
clouds and glances up, throttle boy, goblet core, salty
skipper . . . In the outdoor café by the chewed stucco
wall and its burgundy flare — a city undressed by
prize light — I can't forget the shape things took —
his chocolate smell — coastal lather — bumping into
each other by shoulder and elbow, secret plumage . . .
roast chilies fuming on the road . . . she embroiders
red and yellow flowers as if the vegetable kingdom
ruled . . . windows, bottles, sunglasses ignited . . . an
old man on the street selling his painting of a town
with no streets . . . pleated vistas . . . rocket me out . . .
liaison to liaison . . .

ALTITUDE

The stone figure's head permanently tilted up — sky watcher — to make an ongoing guidebook — sky writing — or twirl your hoop skirt with appliquéd stars — sky rhymer — and don't you then see the hard facts disintegrate? They put down their pens and looked up . . . ancestral symmetry . . . how you scratch the page to let in light . . . Or was it a crimson dahlia on slow bloom with astral spikes that caught him off guard and so, pierced by a legend he couldn't refute, he scooped up what remained of his story of the walk through the park and though fundamentally stripped *by a red marauder* reconstituted his ligatures and restrung his silhouette grid so that the glare was reflected back sliver by sliver and his friend saw only the outer shape of the crisp black veil . . . Where do you look and how do you look? 2,500 BC Anatolia a carved figure labeled "star-gazer." I put on my blue smock coat for a walk, swing my hands in the patch pockets . . . rooftops, treetops, hilltops, skyline . . . the distance between two steps expands as I pick up speed. In the notch of a lifted step as if floating . . . *volador* . . .

JOHN SAID . . .

Sprawled before us full of meaning but which alphabet
in — is that you on the bed arms up, legs up, eyes up? —
to make a bouquet of parts — sheared by the fluttering
bamboo blinds — are those my boots on the flat-weave
rug, solemn as tombstones yet glistening like loam? —
where the jade plant in its fat gold pot is magnet to the
afternoon air that ladles on the . . . is that your nose ring
flashing signals, recumbent decoder . . . ? My tipped
vault opens onto African kente cloth splashed on the
mattress that is by chance his extract and froth . . . A
memory dispatch signs-in just as the word "galloping"
is mouthed . . . with E in Brazil tucked in a feral crouch
and J in DF thick with morning hair and . . . Is it you,
spindle, unreeling *filament, filament, filament* in the heat
of disclosure tactile attaching invention anew as face-to-
face *totally* occupying space, *inhabiting* space . . . ?

SAGACITY

Look at the past, that conduit of vapor — she squints at the window as if rummaging through time — mumbling something about "my body . . ." — patina flows — redistributed flank . . . Each morning as she works at her desk the cramped hand and its . . . or the influx of his muscular smile as he used to . . . a still point on a revolving globe, a spoon of hours . . . the little silver cat wiggled free of her lap, licked his stretched paw — (if she could lick her paw!) — and forgot the previously-to-die-for strokes . . . She got up and stretched as best she could, prickly fingers . . . an influx of where she was, the immediate coordinates of the sunlit room, ivory walls, sloping floor, baskets and painted pots, the open ledger, the notebook splayed like a specimen; a clatter to attention as if cramming down meatballs or toasted nuts or big fists of runny cheese, if she could seize them and fix them, if she could lock the melodious facts in place . . . She stood still in the gale of objects and signs like a mast, sucked at the wind, crossed her arms, stared down a yellow bowl, *dared* it to fade . . .

CONSTRUCTOR

Panned into view the way a story gets told: first the
hat, then the long neck, then the fireplug torso, then
the pointed shoes with their surprise recursive tips. I
thought, "Some kind of spillover may be necessary..."
And sure enough this character fled over the cloister
walls red cheeked in a rippling nightie — gothic cen-
terfold — fueled by hearsay he himself had whispered
— and disappeared in a puddle of gelatin light with
hem raised tenderly to show off his fine, burnished
ankles and help detail the image of flight . . . I put
down the book with its gold-crusted letters, fanned
the pages like a man impatient to be hurt and forgive
— requiem itch — a ready sack of eulogies, beneficent
looks, palliative strokes — checking off nicknames, old
addresses, assignation dates . . . I wanted to make an
animal out of sheets and air with the brush of a wand;
I wanted to hang labels on limp bodies and file them
for occasional resuscitation; I wanted to watch the
jiggling drawers open and close — master maker —
and take notes on the twitching parts — crisp shins,
stubby thumbs, big toothy grins — with names like
Saxophone Boy and Velvet Growler and New Elonga-
tor and Camembert Man already printed in purple ink

on 3 x 5 index cards in a neat pile on the table . . . the augury of phrases . . . shivering silence . . . *made me from dead; raaaarrgh!*

HELIOS CREAM

Wiped it out, just wiped out the desk — scaffolding dismantled — in the helios cream of 9 A.M. — ornament air — if air could shower or flood — wiped out the cylinder seals, the belligerent calculator, the bottomless tray with its unanswered letters, broken knobs, chopped shards, mushroom tips and grinder ash . . . Who was sitting with his back to the window, a wedge in molten light, as the bedposts flickered and the book spines faded in the wavering grid, the foaming scarlet drapes bled out — vanish swagger — memento by memento released . . . Perched on the prong of a giant tremor he scrambled to attention and shook his head like a tambourine. How many thirsty words flew out of his wide-open mouth? With lips flapping like gathering wings he clambered up the rock pile, clausal, operatic, replete. *In the courtyard at midnight at midnight* I listened to his warble and wail, calibrating the measures that would unwrap and unleash me: choral orthography, archival vanishing points, pointillist clover, voluble lullabies, lapidary fishtails, thrumming abrasions, floral contingencies, radial timbres, crackle, fissure, stitch, and brine . . . I held my face in a gash of light and went under . . .

MY DEMOCRACY

Where do you look and how do you look? Architects in doorways — bombshells of cryptic shrubbery — to catch a ripple and go Delphic . . . One small orchid perfuming the whole room, green leopard-skin flippers and purple skirt: applause! Sap on the trees in the morning gleam: mercury light. Into your brown eyes magnetic climbing a trellis of rubbed skin, maneuvered into place, ascendant socket . . . If we are revelers, ordinary shoulders and hips; if the acrobatic blankets yanked back reveal primary apparatus — versatility bulb — stammering ballads and blues — in the jangling pride or no-pride close-up — reciprocal fraternity — it clarifies attention, of this regard, within a palpable frame, honing and homing, relaying focus, *without edifices or rules* a mutual institution, snug as citizens . . .

MORTAL CITY

Shivering in the evidence, a marionette's ballooning knees, flap of mouth . . . and then the strung necklace will be loosed of pearls . . . wreathes around me as transfiguration — scattered organza — wrecked in the pumpkin-mobile — such dizziness in the centrifugal pull when the shadow mantra spins on a polished desk — swept into the dark conch reserved for golden boys — where I have addressed you as *Signor* in evening gloves on a high C — simian yodel, that — with spectators showering down blown kisses converted into exit signs . . . And there you are with my jerking body laid in your lap on a patchwork quilt, speaking me easy, inhaling all my knowledge and skill like a vacuum . . . of which I had been or become in a beautiful flourish of intention and surrender . . .

WAVE

Really on a broomstick after quarry, like a poet drunk
on vowels . . . thrashing among the tousled clouds . . .
ceremony of innocence as high heart . . . billowing as
the fervor swells or fades. With a proffered hand's tidal
pull — magnetic pelt — you tumble onto my trundle
bed, into the spool of the night we call Rolling Au-
rora . . . in our silent language of shudders and ticks,
where sleep burrows even as we whisper "hello." And
you can read all about the adventures of Nimbus and
Flutter, ensconced in a pillowy nook of yarn-ends and
off rhymes, slumberous vigil . . . Then: golden coher-
ence as the third hour breaks open and the painting on
the back wall comes to life, with its pendants and glob-
ules and aqua miasma shedding blue . . . in a lustrous
stucco room rubbed up by concomitant breathing . . .
flickering candle of the eyes . . . disposition and axis . . .
as if we might actually say what we see and see what we
say . . . crest and trough . . . flowing together . . . who
may approximately live forever . . .

ODE

An empty wagon flares on the hillside. Vapors of objects in procession — (they had held them and felt them to be real) — candle, basket, hammer, plum — as shadow-thrones in a line of sight . . . Variable rays . . . How do you touch and where do you touch? She puts on her helmet and goggles, she will race through charged space until she slams into something — plastered emporium — and bring down the scented garden whole. Emblems blurt their secrets in a rush — a flotilla of doffed hats — revving into full disclosure, surrender relish. How our tipsy heads bob as we swallow boxes, ox-es and x-es! Stampede for the purple manzanita swirling, the ruby laptop and the Sterling spoon cast from a twig . . . The night was convivial and the conversation flowed. She was calmly explaining her theory of perceptual preeminence, soothed by warm noodles and baked roots, relative guises . . . An empty wagon flared on the hillside . . .

EL DESEO

Where did he go when he couldn't say — spire or pla-
teau — when the elastic alphabet vaulted beyond his
will or way — he wanted to — nomad with sand in his
hair — he wanted to — tumbled in or out of bed with
sleep in his eyes, moths winging — he wanted to — a
litany of origins, crescendos, divagations, loose ends,
open ends, signs and signposts — he wanted not so
much *to* say as know *how* to say and *what* to say — in the
hot groan of afternoon that pressed him in and jacked
him up — floating but tethered — his flask of lips closed
to himself but open to me — though he wanted to —
hands raking my hair, whisk of his breath, amulet eyes,
as the drawn yellow curtains fluttered and heaved and
the pink walls flashed — I wanted to . . .

IN THE DOME

In truth it was the flask of the sky I put to my lips like
a castaway, from the ridge of the patio lookout, palm
fronds clashing, the salmon-stucco belltower with its
great pendulous bell — I wanted to — and the clouds
whisked across in flat sheets, streaming plateau, until
suddenly the hot blue sky flares and the hot thick air
falls with its litany of parrot screech, clanging gate, en-
gine cough — I wanted to — where you can feel the
still-restless, saturated turf shift underfoot, and wait for
the great tumbling rain to free the next generation of
buried moths in a whispered frenzy — plate shards and
fabric shreds, moon-white pumpkin seeds and flutter-
ing corn husks — I wanted not so much to *say* as be
said to — rotating sonar . . . elastic alphabet . . . amulet
ears — in the torrid mix of wind and dust and rusty gui-
tar, a swirling vault of pressed voices, untold clasps — I
wanted him to . . .

EDGE OF LIGHT

Where can you say or when can you say and who can
you say it to — he nearly did — fragments of speech,
nomad body parts tumbled on the verge — he needed
to — moths in darkness, but floating towards — he
couldn't yet — in the flamboyant heat that grilled him
and which he sparked — knowing the gestures and
moves — elastic innocence — but not the shape or how
to punctuate — skidding origins — or that the women
in the square and circling through the streets weighed
down by piles of colored cloth strapped to their shoul-
ders might not carry *his* name stitched there in silver
thread, embroidered litany — he could almost — from
the plateau of the unmade bed — a flask of tequila at
hand to burn back the rising words — amulets each, but
only if strung — his hands outseeing his eyes by miles
— vaulted arches, quivering spires — and me breathing
into his mouth, "You will, you will, you will . . ."

AN ARCHEOLOGY

and the fine ribs of the chairs playing the wind, the wind, the wind . . . shaken the morning . . . gasping through thick, shiny leaves at night, pulling the hair of the wind, the wind . . . hulls of worn bodies — take my swollen hands — the blue drifting toward yellow and white — skeleton pebbles — seethes among the pleasure seekers — grain by grain, finer than dust . . . I curl on the foam mat in the whirling grind in my unitard skin, removable as a sleeve of silk, while the bleached fronds flay at the wind, the wind, my fingers play at the wind . . . Or if on a bright day bone light stripped down though *Dido will not dissolve . . . into sleep* . . . she will dissolve . . . into wind . . . Inside the belly of the harbor, pitched forward to seize the incline in a gust . . . as if filling sails . . . with my gray beard and gray hair churning . . .

PLUME

Transfixed to the, by the, on the congruities, who is her-
self a vanishing point coming to closure — dusky flutter
— trilling away like a watchdog on drugged sop, chan-
neling her mother and grandmother who've engraved
on her locket phrases in script: "glide on a blade" and
"rustling precedes the shuck." This is not my teeming
fate, my rind, my roiling ellipsis or valedictory spray of
myrrh. Always it's morning, afternoon or evening —
the loot of hours — a magic sack grasping vacuum but
heavy in the hand, and from which, together, we pull a
swarm of telepathic bees, melons beached in a green bin,
a lithograph of the city from its crumbling ramparts,
crackled pitchers and the mouth of a cave. Perhaps this
is my open weave, my phantom rialto or plume of light.
We bow to each other in the mash of flickering things.
We are completely surrounded.

II.

Gather

GATHER

A specimen, a set of eyes, a whiff from the fountain-head . . . If the room is a frame and the frame is a window and the window set in an arcade of options: amoebic rustle, stammered marrow, incarnation kettle . . . The air stops, except for a few jets of birdsong — cactus wren, thrasher. Where does the song begin or end in the audible hush? Threads of a cortex, sticky like a new web. Quivering aroma. You can hear the dogs bark at 6:15, agitated by the appearance of things and the distant trot of wild pigs. And here come the swine, fat and balletic, shaggy torpedoes on delicate shins, whipping the dogs into a froth as they skirt the fence and head for the brush: gnarly tumbleweeds . . . apparitional stubble . . . The sky is already icy clear, cloudless, fuel for projection. From his burrow under thick blankets, steaming coffee at his cuff: a set of eyes . . . a specimen . . .

CIRCUIT

Let's say the air crackled with static as the pink morning — the orange morning — settled down, raising the bleached high-grass, the tangled spurts of black mesquite, hurling the fence posts higher and cauterizing the blue hills . . . Then the household dream with its household trim stiffened the petunias in their pot — compass trumpets — indigo listeners — as the small corridor lengthened and the ruddy carpet rolled its stripes . . . She stretched her arms, twisted her back, flung herself on the paisley couch where a trickle of sun hit the pillow, a plunge into abstraction . . . Who *were* the dream-men last night, the profile with its owl eye, the beautiful zigzag scar throbbing, the pure staccato speech clipping voiced words into geometric shapes that hovered, crystalline, discrete . . . ? She tried to form a conduit, cupping her hands. She was hungry to snatch such formed phrases from the fully charged air — alligator antennae — a century ahead and *be* their shape and sentience, writhing senses . . . An early breeze rocked the siding. She could feel the swept distances invade her. "I," she said out loud, "am," she said, "a preface" . . . A violet scar pulsed.

THE OPENING AIR

A searchlight obelisk, a suction stick — lightning hits the desert wind wheel all night, spitting elbows of fire . . . as if in one flash and one flash we see the whole picture: a trailer done up as a cabin, a wooden porch for a glade, two plum trees: the woods . . . gingerly a living space — tincture of the domestic — vis-à-vis the shawl of stars — nudged into place — loop of icons: decorative pot, throw rug, basket and window sash — as a grotto in the vast cave of opening air, vistas of vistas . . . Do we go or stay, cuddle in the den or blast out on a gust of heat . . . ? where the windswept valley and its faraway mountain crust . . . who we are and who we may become . . . on a continuum slant of diminishing border . . . as if standing, or melting, or being, or seeing, or floating or soaring or sighing or willing . . . and the panorama sightlines and skylines *so* near . . . and the images dusty *and* clear — meridian flyway — and the great, sizzling bolts of light . . . !

[SONG]

The sky is not my startled face, my molten hive, my
thrashing cape . . . It's not my milky piano, my hissing
shield or thatch of white, my turret or my slash. I turn
at the fence and head back home. Perhaps it *is* an ingot
of light, a wheeling node, a crystal ram. It may well be
my deliveryman, my mogul swarm, a catapult saloon,
my flannel hide or arc of flight, my majesty powder or
helmet of night, my millennial stash, my open at last,
my vertical stew, my vagabond blue . . .

THE STILLNESS

Once I was a sailor in a town with no name — hey nonny nonny or go cat go — I had a red mountain bike and two skateboards — wheel confetti — but my skiff was my über-pal. I could split the seam of any vector — river, lake or draw — with coots sputtering from mangrove jumbles, surprised by my sudden proximity — and the imprint of my oar in the liquid sky barely visible . . . Some called me Micah Glint and some called me Mary Louise and both were fine with me, depending on which shoes I wore, sleek rubber or nubby hemp, woven in strips or knit from fallen leaves . . . I could cut through downtown squat in the slats, as low and clean as a needle . . . gravel showers parting . . . clattering, gray canyon air . . . Once I was a sailor with my long hair flowing, with a satchel of pink apples and a bouquet of peas, tendrils trailing . . . in a stub of an afternoon removed from sequence . . . heretic hovercraft . . . in a flat eddy where you watched from the shore or corner or car or chair . . . to whom I waved relentlessly as I glided past, uncoiling my way in circles or arcs such as cursive letters make . . . in that gap, in that rounded space, in my silent groove like a paper boy in a paper boat turning as I was turning . . .

[COWBOY, DON'T . . .]

Cowboy, don't eat me. Yes I'm tasty, yes I've come from my warren stuffed like a Christmas goose, tongue lolling. But cowboy, think of my varnished nose, my bucket of pink gums, the opera of my eyes. Let the knotted grid loosen, let your hard silhouette overflow — alluvial redemption — let me slink away soundlessly into the lavender hills — sanctuary caravan — cowboy, don't eat me, go for the calf over there, tender as cactus jelly. I'm *too* sweet and *too* fat, my innards are frescoes of hormone spikes and acid splats — *mucho* digestive scrabble — don't open me to the scouring winds, please, close your paring knife, your dripping cowboy lips . . . Life is episodic and a revolution idles, there behind the pink escarpment where my pack is gathering now . . . The world, *este mundo immenso*, gyrates and kicks, and the hot stars *in their pale ignition* are burning . . . burning . . .

THE WAYS

Ribbons of snow in the mountains . . . She wants to augment her archive of rocks . . . oscillates between looking up and looking down and looking down and looking down . . . beveled thrusts of milky quartz, corrugated rifts of malachite, radium green . . . a few flat plates for the patio, some monoliths for the garden rim . . . Tectonic custodian — she studies embedded crystals or copper sheen . . . gathers her ground . . . Tall sycamore branches etched white against a gray mist, propellers of the rising light . . . But he is spinning in place before the high relief of the crackled bark of an alligator juniper . . . Commander of signs — he relishes the fractured ridges to turn a page in their configuration, testing: *checkerboard fissures . . . quake skin . . . moon arbor . . . blistered tunic . . . coruscated char . . . geode couturier . . . igneous trunk . . .*

GLORIA MUNDI

Once I was an old man with wind in his hair — pulver-
ized by the air — that wasn't fair so I crawled back over
the bridge *to where the beautiful nights dance like bears* —
and sidling up to the Professor of Youth who was seeth-
ing to see me unspooled — tamped furrows — sat down
in my former spot with a heft of purpose . . . and with
my eyes now sparkling like fresh cream started to sing,
"Attention purifies the vagrant mind" as if it had been
peeled out of a hymnal from my childhood . . . Once
I was a Young Turk with wind at his back — it was
hard to argue with *that* . . . Once I had a tunic of cobalt
blue, a twilight cape, a dark kimono . . . with a sweep
of authority as if it were my hair I climbed the laddered
air to where the voices hung like ornaments in cobalt
space — dancing bears — and waited in the sonic arches
as if I were at home there and learned my methods and
honed my craft . . . Bridge and arch, ladder and stair . . .
happily at home there . . .

CITIZEN

Across the wide rim of the Bay — cirrus — hissed equanimity — the glass cutter's cascade — where he will pause to locate himself on a map of *monarchs and queens* — in the city's periodic swirl that leaves him lolling on wobbly knees — across the lumpy pavement and rain gullies just filled — artery from café to bookstore to hill-park — where he will dangle yet again as from a descending parachute but fall no farther nor more quickly because so fascinated by the raucous air in a shaft of time — across that flipped metropolis on its back ventral skin laid bare to him — where he will follow his newly stumbling gait as if running behind himself as he once was in the high cram of simultaneous days — twister — which he has been, and longed for, and stampeded into, duly imagined, communalized, extracted from, recollected, remade, revisited, abided by, grown into and old in and smart from and stayed fresh for — crossing and re-crossing — and watches still — cirrus — wide across the wide rim of the Bay . . .

STATION

Sat in front of the window box speckled with narration — cotyledon turbine, etc. — looking for a twitch in the soil — pattern repository — or the periscope of morning . . . Made a new city, then, a jumble of colored houses down a hillside — to stand up and go out and walk along — in another tongue, resistant, fertile, florid idiom — clustered torches — flash . . . Talked, then, hammered by stuttering silences but mouthing thick consonants like fresh bread, a distant calculus of yeast and sound — listened from the trembling core *the mute still air* stirred — template drift — generation — as if of spring . . . speaking . . .

THE FUTURE PRESENT

The trees outside the latticed window reflected in the
mirror, and in the glass of the framed print . . . slurred
the coordinates of place — thrashed prism — as she
watched the lozenges of light compete . . . In the glare
of the clash of surface and depth — jeweled inconti-
nence — she couldn't be sure which space she faced was
inside, which was outside, lost in the warp of the shift-
ing stack, a jog in the axis, a blur of planes . . . She
understood the game . . . with only a little squirm sur-
rendered her calculations, gave up her precious idea of
order, and lay herself into the fist of the chair like a prac-
ticed rocketeer, loosely forward, eyes brimming, ready
to go . . .

INTERLUDE

The platform of the novel — say Zola's unbuckled stage — hunkered down on the slope of the couch — combusting personae — they rise from the amniotic bracelet calling each other's name . . . whose puffy lips — orbital rosebud — close over mine; whose moorings lock on my terror and need; whose margins my ethical trough; whose innocence my crushed head . . . and the sphincter of the plot unmolding us — the quarry, the elemental ore — where I stretch, propped up on my arm, squinting *and* gaping, unable/unwilling to sleep — in pages . . . in pages . . .

ERASER

There would be days when, work over — rumpled champion — he'd fling himself into the walk home like a whirlpool, tilting with the swaying pines, wobbling to the uneven growl of buses and trucks, banked in gyration as the ever-scouting hawks shrieked . . . A cream of receptor cells: He wanted maximal permeation, curiosity elevation, variety pollination . . . as he neared his house the more buoyed he was by sensory incursions the less attached to the geology of his name; the more dogwalkers barked and basketballers whooped — accidental punctuation — the less he clung to his own worn phraseologies . . . He began to chant in nonsense hexameters like a sleepwalker in the grip of nocturnal idioms — nursery rhymes and formula rhythms — aroused to a sustained attention that also resembled waking up . . . He wanted to be a sponge re-distributor, a dissolution bride — listening, watching — on a prodigal stroll that unmade him by pride of surrender and wiped him clean . . . ambulatory tutorial . . . to finally lie down at apex spread-eagled and splayed . . . in saturation refuge . . . just *taken* . . .

THEN

Once we were in the loop . . . slick with information
and the luster of good timing. We folded our clothes.
Once we stood up *before* the standing vigils, *before* the
popping vats, *before* the annotated lists of marshaled
forces with their Venn diagrams like anxious zygotes,
their paratactic chasms . . . *before* the set of whirligig
blades, modular torrent. We folded our clothes. Once
we remembered to get up to pee . . . and how to pee
in a gleaming bowl . . . soaked as we were in gin and
coconut, licorice water with catalpa buds, golden beet
syrup in Johnny Walker Blue and a beautiful blur like
August fog, cantilevered over the headlands . . . We
tucked into the crevices of the mattress pad twirling
our auburn braids, or woke up at the nick of light and
practiced folding our clothes. Our pod printed head-
bands with hourly updates, announcing the traversals of
green-shouldered hawks through the downtown loop,
of gillyfish threading the north canals, of the discov-
ery of electron calligraphy or a new method of wash-
ing brine. We smoothed our feathers like birds do, and
twitched ourselves into warm heaps, and followed the
fourth hand on the platinum clocks sweeping in arcs
from left to right, up and down, in and out . . . We

were steeped in watchfulness, fully suspended, itinerant floaters — ocean of air — among the ozone lily pads and imbrex domes, the busting thickets of nutmeg, and geode malls. At night we told stories about the future with clairvoyant certainty. Our clothing was spectacular and fit to a T. We admired each other with ferocity.

ASCENDANT

"Let it come, Jhoan," I said, "empty the cylinders" . . .
as if in the twitch of a dream, as if the milky manna
flowed from a spigot, as if the moist cleft and the upcast
eyes presented themselves on a table or desk for degus-
tation or the eighty-eight rules of prosody . . . How do
you talk *to*, how do you aim for the ear . . . ? So set him
down on the tip of my honeyed pen — stirring billows
— winsomely tidal — where the diastolic breakers curl
— and looking him straight in the tank whispered: "the
labials tug, the plosives stun, the linguals gather you
in . . ." But I was already chuffing like a marathon run-
ner deep in the trough — spattered luster — my exhor-
tations came back on me, spinning in the other direc-
tion: "the plosives *defend*, the labials *yearn*, the linguals
surrender" . . . ah . . . I saw an unlaced man on a slat-
ted trellis climbing like jasmine, flagrant as heliotrope.
Though he was too tall and too fast and decorated with
too many blinking lights — comet trail — I clambered
up *to where the beautiful nights dance like bears*, foothold
by shaky grasp, pocked by a cascading shower of sparks
and holistically tingling . . . helium fuse-box . . . ascen-
dant gaga serenade . . . empyrean tremens . . .

COMPASS

Where the clattering tiles of the patchwork paths — marimba walkway — as he wobbles through the squealing heat — ceremonial hoops — with a loaf of onion bread under arm and a bouquet of pink carnations tied like a string of oaths still quivering . . . hill-light across the tumbling cubes of houses . . . performative city . . . in a stupor of pleasure he scans and measures how to get lost, and which passage up which sloping stair will reveal the fabled Jhoan, trailing his shadow like a mermaid's tail . . . into the quenching . . . as if a day lengthened by stretching in the middle — globe of hours — he loops outward, adrift but unwavering . . . spun commander . . . and *farther, farther, farther sail* . . .

BRUJA

Alcove of the shade tree, under which they neck and whisper . . . and gather their tribe. She stencils the tilt of their heads from her perch on the iron bench, their dreamy eyes and smiles. Migrating neurons: It's as if a baton streaking the air laid them bodily onto her page . . . In the mounting embrace there in the Plazuela Obregon under a fresh puff of filtering clouds she slips their oyster into her shell — among the milling Sunday throng — what she's been waiting for — on the edge of the bezel that is her acquiring art — like a dusty hatbox suddenly filled with living pulp — fluted swells — in a brazen reversal of nostalgia . . . She is their growing stalk, their link, their flowering rod, their helix tunnel and their watering hole. They are her guardian foil, her carnal frame, her forgiven stitch, her undertow and magnum light. Connected silently bench to bench, shadow to shadow, spark to spark, they arc and flow, flow and arc . . .

PROPORTIONAL

A beige dog, his sleek nose tangled in the odors of the street, conjuring hours past — elixir — as a simultaneous influx of beautiful strangers . . . redolent streamers . . . To inhale the stone and veined oak, the green and ochre walls, tapering alleys, to coax the fluid out . . . ! Well, it poured for an hour ripening into hail — articulated rush and drum — the bouncing ice inside a rattling torrent of rain . . . scrawled through the swiveling canyon such astounded names as mythic plagues are drawn from . . . curated then for me a further spectacle cupped by my glass door watching and listening pure unrestrainable excess . . . invincible roar . . . inhaling *me* . . . of the little serenade, the miniature stance, the tiny thunderstruck eyes . . .

AND IF AT 4 P.M.

No ghosts, no backlighting, no Zen thump — but maybe a telepathic swish. No teased subtext, no demarcated key, stirred cauldron or lunge of query. Maybe a seething clavicle, a trembling cadence flushed . . . Not his sealed capsule — no good — or the sharp cusp of his alternate names. A trickle, a sputter, a nugget in the pocket unburnished, a caracole of distant clues . . . I'm at my desk in the park inside my apartment of a strange city at home in the square . . . I looked into the blue-gray eyes of a tender man who asked me to look, please — no jostled frame or tightened armature at crook. A kind of metabolic transparency, yes, an unexpected chime like the clink of glasses already half drunk, a quick shudder, and the turns of a tremulous coil . . . inward to pleasure . . . inward to sense . . . !

SCOUT

Rippled purr — with a shrug I fling myself under the table — fetal tangle — potion jammed in each fist — down the lexicon in a shape-shifting gulp — where a café on the Bridge of Owls joins the ancient in-road to the city's center . . . tremor of epochs . . . a sanctioned fable of days . . . You can stretch your hands, wing-man, and touch the leaning houses on opposite sides, flaring orange, mauve, and blue like an aviary . . . the street pitched vertical, winding narrow, a wisp of direction for this convergence . . . to fill in the cracks, sink underpinnings wide as lake beds, set the ravine to humming. I put down my luggage — such an unintended mountain of cracked teacups and wicker bibs, alpaca bedrolls and silicone boots! — to spread the surging city before me, a vast net of firing pins, constellation magi . . . as I lie on my side with measured breath . . . this murmuring atlas, swarm of inflections, this hot particle flood . . . and follow . . .

III.

Hive

CANTO JONDO

This is not a swansong. I'm living the quiver. Once I rotated like an awl, boring into . . . or felt the awl, punctured and prepared, twist of surrender. Where are you opened and how are you opened . . . ? The Great Sprawling, The Great Contraction: We felt the vibrations in our eyelids — folding fan of the iris — seeing and stampeding and guzzling the broth of things — and we have heard the busting rhymes at midnight. A feast of seeming: This may well be my conjurer's spree . . . Once I had an exit wound, teeming with the will of the people. It was savory pie to Chac Mool, who served me with lychee paste and mescal dew, a drink named Bleeding Waters. I was not his swansong — though he tried to stanch the flow. How do you thread a sigh so it attaches to the sky and rises like a mind on fire? Perhaps this *is* my sculpted stone in high relief . . . a whack of light. They called me Harrowing Esplanade but walked right through with soft little dogs on catgut leashes and plastic bags to catch their dropped endearments. They called me Aleatory Jackpot and I broke their backs — their banks — their stack of books . . . I am riveted to easy solutions and complex elisions, like a soft little dog in heat. Once I began every story with, "Once . . ." You are my exit wound, pure and translucent, a suction, a quiver. This is my swansong.

UNCONTAINABLE

As morning settled she watched the petal of the over-
blown lily — orange cream — fall like a fledgling —
snatched by the small thicket of ferns — and simmer
there. She saw light scroll across the floor, transform
the splatter pattern from blue to near-white, and white
walls kneading blue out of their shadows. She watched
from her chair as she had learned to do, gasping at each
shift of color and line — vamping materium — shed-
ding contour and fill — retooled her own sense of pur-
pose and form — crackling in her thorax or rustling in
her spine — as if her inner membranes had been pricked
and the soft tissue torn free and some amoebic assonance
transferred her to this bath of objects in transition . . .
She bowed to the charity of light in her corner as her
conversions spread she fed on slatted chairs more slat-
ted, pleated drapes more deeply creased . . . red cushions
gushing . . . and now the uncontainable lilies as though
she'd bridled at tedious common sense and in a spew let
fly her own . . . curling jet . . . her backflip aurora . . .
her upward peeling splash, sprung lunge *scintille* . . . she
shuddered and shook with each iteration in the elemen-
tal room she occupied in the middle of May . . . apricot
eucharist spillover *jeté* . . . !

THE ABUNDANCE

Surely these people have found their way, with their buttered pavilions and feathered ecliptics, their family dioramas and migrated skins, their anodyne flatbread and renegade sauces shot with voltage and thickened by erasure . . . For sure this city is a threshold in play, with its excavated courtyards layered by shade, its alleys of lost stratagems and scuttling students charmed by digressions, its pastel stacks and glistening facet high on the hill that is my blue box that is my citadel unearthed each morning that is my fugitive reconstruction, elevated, breathless again — totemic vista — on this incline in the clamorous hive . . .

SUCH MEASURE

Hello, old friend. Curtain up on our past — you look
like a sprig on the old trunk — cranial arcade through
which we retrace . . . de-accelerator — Hello again,
with your chrome foot-brace and pneumatic knees, with
my pressed-wafer smile and overripe Rembrandt eyes
— hurled periodicity — bumping into you — when
we plunged through the coral, sleek as seal pups; we
thrashed with the dancing monkeys and wore them
out . . . Hello, skating in place; hello, smashed atom;
hello, planks across dark water . . . Remember I taught
you the four basic flounces, the ribbon sonata, the ac-
cordion walk? You showed me the peg-leg slider, the
jumping pulpit and the wet parade . . . now among the
glass windbreak, wood benches and flower boxes — you
could pull apart the air with your teeth — in a Friday
lull — we talk in discrete turns . . . such measure . . .
inexorable pride . . . that had torn open rooms in space
torn open lungs torn open breath . . .

THE WORK

If I had language I would build a kiosk on the hill, a
clubhouse of inflection and glide — indicative pivots —
You know that spot by the big bay tree with its matador
arms and deep shade of ardor? You could have a key too
to the vibrating lock with spit in the hole like a sun leak-
ing through the leaves to juice the inner sanctum . . . If
I had such dignity as mendicant words would confer —
with my tonsure and empty stare, my alphabet envy and
émigré zeal — we could take to my hut in an upsurge of
chatter, flourishing our syncopated tongues like épées
to the very minimal point — acrobatic focus in the silver
glint and slash — wrapped up *in the living changes of syn-
tax* . . . Then, maestro: gusto . . . contour . . . shivering
fill . . . mouth of the hand, hand of the eye . . . a box on
a hill, or a lung, or a sign . . . and the pure cold body of
glee set free . . . or a line . . .

FLAT ON A MAP

And if they'd risen from their mattresses on the downtown street in a vapor-cloud of old flannel — crushing comfort — if they'd wedged themselves forward through the gauntlet of doctors' thumbs, fragrant in their plaid suspenders . . . draped across the polished steps like something dropped in terror and haste . . . She squints into the future city, a narrator leaning on a verb (she's standing on the curb) as the mottled sky, fog-swirled, throbs and releases, hectoring the pigeons with alternating flares of black and white . . . "There is consequence," she thinks — inbound catcalls — massive accidental lockup — she crosses to the library squat in gray light like a tugboat — "There is circulating cause and effect," (the library's closed on Wednesday.) Peeling back the fence, the rockslide, the brooding incredulity . . . she wanders home while the streetlights start to phosphoresce . . . whisper of blankets rolled over . . . the silent cage of nightfall . . . not speaking not looking as she passes . . . key in hand turns back to eye the skyline, half lit . . . relative breath, relative air, relative sleep . . .

INSTEAD OF AN ARIA

Blended elasticity — the way a day follows a day — I
pull off my shoes to smooth the transition like a guppy
slipping into shallows . . . Staggered before me: unread
monographs, random URLs, six imperative toaster aids
and a spotted banana emeritus . . . How will I choose
which news to use, crouched by the rack with my scis-
sors aloft at compositional zenith . . . ? Scoop by scoop
I identify the incoming measures to put them in their
place: thunk of colliding cars on the corner, rumors
of Iranian fission, the mushroom butter sizzling, Ma-
rio purring my name, my name . . . A melody array.
A further opening field . . . Sprinkle of sun through
the dirty windows — leopard-print light — archipelago
on the Zapotec rug — I'll lay down among the woven
stripes and streaming dots . . . in my skin sled going no-
where . . . made of nothing, made of air . . . arms spread
wide . . . *cantador* . . .

IMMEDIATE LEGEND

How did I find you where you found me? (congenital relish.) Where were you headed when I became you? (ponytail cabochon.) The shift is epochal — sealed into the seams of what's written — stretched across the horizon like a quilt of pixels — where you stand akimbo stained by sauces — (pliable ruby) — how did I catch your light in my mouth? (caramel samovar . . .) A pulley system raising chin or ass — yanked in — grommet eyes — your grin flushed out as your hand clutches . . . I watch the pleated curtain swell . . . which is my fourth act . . . my icing on the . . . your polyglot moans, my responder, your braising, my ricochet stick, your bed of clover, my nutrient — *this blows my heart* — Last Meal I scarf down un-condemned . . . !

THE CORRESPONDENCES

Puckered velvet — I mean the skin of the moon — I
mean the Great Plains at dusk — I mean his vertebrae
in quiet sleep . . . or the flat cloud cover seen from the
plane SF/Vancouver to the edge of the world . . . How
do you expose the spokes, shining like many eyes; how
do you make the confluence clear . . . ? The Douglas fir
was so tall the high-rise condos drooped, submerged in
their blue transparencies, glassy aquifer . . . It was shirt-
sleeve warm as they walked the urban sea wall, span-
ning the smiles of passing men, marking their giveaway
gestures: flapping tassels . . . Prodded each other to lis-
ten and look, to name the enveloping parts: a building's
checkerboard tiles, another's sculpted ship in low relief,
the garden's chatty foxgloves, a jogger's ginger hair . . .
as though the necklace of formed things had come un-
strung in their hands and every rotating bead — mol-
ecule balloon — had a label attached that needed to be
spoken out loud — facets of a flicker — so they talked
— as if arm in arm by saying . . . in Northwest late-light
afternoon reverberation . . . in quick notation . . . in
relation . . .

[SONG]

The sky's a mound of abalone dust . . . it's not my lucid
tube, my high blue finial, my true believer, my gallant
swain in tow, my lubricating who (or two), my thun-
derbird corral, my rising thrall . . . I transfer buses by
the falafel stand and shrug . . . It's just a bank of dun,
a moisture slink, a muffler thick as whale skin, pond
of croaking frogs, bowl of glue, my gumball crest, my
silent goad, my wretched haircut for thirty bucks, my
congee road . . . I cross the street, look up, and scratch
my chin . . . Perhaps it really *is* my shadow hat, my rusty
talking stick or fitted coat of mail, my steward of duty,
my last illusion test, a low canoe that's slicing through,
my second chance in time . . . my hanging rhyme . . .

AGAIN

We tug at our shirttails (down) and belt loops (up) — gravity's analog — and test the wind with our index fingers pointed to Halifax. We say goodbye to the silent peaks that scorched our dreams — North Periscope and Dry Forever — nod to the scattered bones of the house, portentous like snakes in shade — to snatch an image from the air in 3D and give it steel walls, parquet floor! — and wrap the dried crab strips and oleander gum in parchment tubes we brought from Egypt — our pageant is an atlas — singing travel songs in the basso register only the saddleback tortoises can hear, with their primal somnolence and kettledrum hides, stone hierophants . . . Invades like the morning chill; sweeps the sky like a falling tail section; cleaves the ground like quake boots, iron cleats . . . We have to go and we wanted to go; we needed a change and we were asked to change; we were heaved out and we broke the door down. Together we crack black walnuts and read the telltale folds . . . a continuous ripple of participatory discourse . . . plenitude and solitude . . . the walking stick's resplendent calm . . . to be still in motion, to waver in measure, to center the matrix as it reels . . . with our water helmets and glistening sun cuffs fitted . . . we disable the iris keys and thumbprint codes, powder the threshold and set the ibex free to roam the crag . . . snap the hatch closed . . . in the back seat by the back window — head in the nest of my hands — I watch the dust rise, the jimson weeds slide by, the crystal towers jostle and shift, the ruts unroll . . .

THIRST

The ping of memory — she thought, "water the plants" — and flush with a sense of duty stroked the pallid leaves, doused the roots steaming like marrow, inhaled the gurgling soil, breathy vapors almost vocal — seared her sense of distance, impaled on the variegated yellow/green spears extracting this juice — she clutched the watering can as if it might be snatched, as if she herself might ditch it diving headfirst into the pot to writhe among the sucking things — originators — she could lose scale in an instant doing the household chores — penetrating to be penetrated — where she would fasten her little island, a puzzle shard ready to snap into place, to a rug or a bowl or a rainforest basket or the sere and solemn yucca morsel by mote of her own indefatigable sympathy and will to belong — spherical osmosis — as she fingered the sleek jade plant each plump, glossy segment swollen almost to bursting . . .

THE CONTRACT

The streets — stitched piers — as if the swells under-
ground — and the people melting eventually — pulled
them along — Victorian accents on the cornices and
sentinel palms lining the center divide — in a sling
on the back of the blue metropolis — ushered them
into the crowded rapids where they honed their skills
— citizens — and reared thus to be in constant mu-
tual proximity they thought to marry the city — had
button-front Levis for a dowry, and madras windbreak-
ers, and baskets of hot durian cakes — not scouring the
streets for witnesses but witnessing the streets — grand
canals — gathering vows — by the tall plumes of cedars
and guardian lampposts and the sleepy eyes of the forty-
eighth floor overlooking the sleepless plaza — multifari-
ous euphoria — greedily watching or being watched —
with fog spilling off the mountain velvet summer shiver
— they do . . . we do . . . I do . . .

SANDMAN

Once I was a bucket of opportunity; I went down into
the well — *take me anywhere . . . I walk into you* — had
my fill, was all swoll' up . . . Once I was strapped to
the helm — gone Crete and the Libyan Sea — for the
ichor of lost ways, crushed thyme, echoing rock walls
— alchemical wanderlust — or a sea-cave under cliffs
— igloo marble — and, dripping there: Claudio . . .
Claudio . . . Claudio . . . ! Once I was a stargazing fool
— flint eyes — the machinations of constellations —
stunned to be under the sky again looking again with
my sensor upraised and the dry earth stomped around
me — Karpathos — or my body flattened to a mat by
summer heat — heliotropic smackdown — as the long-
bottled name spewed out: Claudio . . . Claudio . . . In
a cottage at the turnout I boiled dandelion roots, baked
my loaves of taro in the form of a tongue — chimeras —
carved an empty wagon on the hillside and filled it with
axle grease, accidental courtships . . . Once I was young
once I was old, history outran me and I outran it, with a
bucket of fresh topsoil and narcoleptic good will — I'm
running still — bunkhouse champion — eager gripping
tendril — in the whirl of a coo . . . as if on call . . .
who? . . . *Claudio!*

IMMINENT

Opened before him as if a spinning map . . . or a chink in the crested wall . . . where the silent cravings are stored with their names in broken code: Playpal in Mufti from . . . ? Advancing Cordon d'Or for . . . ? He turns over every rock for a stamp of verisimilitude — poet's privilege — puts his hand inside each sheath for the snug omens to release their pitch . . . Who is the messenger with the refresh button approaching from the hood? Is it the usual Autumn Riot, the Character Assassin, the famous Rainbow Slut? Which Zion will he savor when the shattered cradle drops its plum? Threaded by anxiousness, hopping from foot to foot, he dreams of savior, surrender, re-glazing, conjunction, submersion, avowal, *connect* . . . It's enough to feel the map stretch, the mossy wall breached . . . Snatched from pale comfort he bows to greet the smasher . . .

THE PRACTICE

They mistook me for illumination — a revenant in
walking shoes — so I gathered significance and spread
text . . . stood beneath the seven cardinal points with
arms upraised — practical telepathy — in a white paper
suit like a flag of surrender, thunder at my back . . . I was
an open man of the open streets — a burnished sieve of
common purpose — scrawled on walls, thrashed cans
and blasted caps for equivalence. I wasn't alone — the
boulevards teemed with wiggly kids and mooing par-
ents slow as boulders. In the Plaza Palabra on a green
iron bench a grand senora suffered the odes of school-
boys and thugs — smiled behind an opal fan while
they searched for words to match their tumultuous
nights — and all words fit . . . In July — volubility — I
hoarded cherries, catalogued their juices — were they
Rainier, Blood Nut, Royal Ann, Squirrel Heart, Rose-
bud or Bing? — then swallowed them one by one like
detonations . . . initiations . . . In a fever of taxonomy
I followed a squadron of dragonflies right to the van-
ishing point . . . Incarnation is a provisional state, but
stretches outward like noon. For practice, I wallowed
and stretched . . .

TRANSMUTATION SUITE

I.

As if the sky itself were always a page, molded by
the yielding winds — what do you read, how do you
read it? — against a cloudbank, smoldering ladder of
thought . . . and his upturned face splattered with fall-
ing leaves . . . He compacts himself into a wedge, a cone
of muscle by the corner of the corner café, and ponders
dark men with light skin, light men with dark skin, skin
men in the thicket of his bed with its catalogue of arched
backs as they dive into the sky of sheets, pulsating en-
velope . . . A gray dog with flopdoodle ears obsesses on
the café's swinging door . . . A steady stream of steady
riders: the bicycle's equilateral calm . . . In the shade of
the liquidambar trees — whisked colonnade — raises
his head, floats up into the looming . . .

II.

A goblet of coffee — my toasted nimbus — and I take
to the streets — pearly scrim of morning fog — with
the eucalyptus trees wriggling free of their pods — men-
thol buttons — in the dispatch of fall light. Look at my
house! — that blue honeycomb of beveled glass — in
formation on the long block; look at the scarlet splash
of fuchsias on the porch, the symmetry of redwood
beams . . . I'm the cargo of that cult in this hoop of days
I bind to walls and fill with vistas looking out — *through*
the painting, *through* the book, *through* the patterned
rug, emblazoned like a maze — for the squint of atten-
tion brought to bear, a simple spoon of nectar, clarity
medallion, secret door ajar or aperture bouquet . . . ooh,
sentience bubbles as I whistle as I walk . . .

III.

The sky was not her quarry, her index vault or influx
throne, her ornamental nook or private lair. She didn't
go there. She couldn't pick apart the quilt, she stitched
the quilt. She scoured the bowl. She stretched her arms
— the fit was snug — inhaling air she touched the air
— tactile euphony — and thought of neutron wreaths,
or chemical emblem buds — but air was not her foil,
her fresh refill or phantom guise, magnetic alphabet or
image stair . . . Perhaps it *was* her air . . .

IV. [CIRCE OR NOT]

As a frame you are the perfect host, with your corridor
eyes and spray of dancing fingers . . . As a channel I
could sail right into you, bob in the froth . . . Here is my
hand: its harbor well known to travelers, well worn, well
extended — skeleton thread of my endless suction loop
— where I stand by my burrow, foaming — as if an agi-
tated broth were stimulated to excess by the approach
of hunger . . . As a hull you have the perfect curves with
your bisecting plunge of fuzzy hair, smooth hollow,
rounded ribs, sturdy planks . . . so many fine bones . . .
your tethered wrists . . . your trickle of sweat . . . your
squeal of hope . . . my squeal of hope . . .

V.

I might say, "a big hug," and mean, "more adjectives."
I might say, "The view from here is awesome," and
mean, "for whom the woozy planet tilts and overflows."
I could post "mac 'n cheese," but serve a silky stew of
tongue and celery heart — with a spot of orchid cream
to quiet the tongue and still the heart . . . It's a warm,
sunny day full of blushing sonorities, shameless as a dis-
co ball — for "semantic density" I offer the back forty,
with its seed rows of mortal glitter, and peach-orchard
caravan bound for Tulsa or Tunis . . . The crowd gasps
as I leap from the margin of error into the sea of change;
a surface wrinkle is a twinkle from below . . . Shower
down, fiesta lexis in excelsis — the forecast for tomor-
row is *saturated* . . .

THE ADVENTURE

Thumbing through the miscellany — divination clatter — with its Holstein cows like calico hills, its bluebell swards and anthracite bluffs, its hidden holding pens with blood-streaked floors . . . I forged ahead, zealously kicking snowballs and gumballs, jumping ravines, leaping rivers, *to where the beautiful nights dance like bears* and spring jets rise to lubricate the skies — clarified mind — veined by horizon lines . . . Take the tissue of this day, our cloak of torpor burst like roe — wild fennel on the air-stream — take the crackle in the sphere, black mint of creosote, the tiny flycatcher's whizz-by flame . . . Here are tins of jellyfish curd we made when we got up and brushed our chestnut hair, and creased our pleated skirts and pants and pinched our cheeks to raise the pink — laid out on placemats with our scribbled names like string pulls . . . conjure wands . . . In a huddle on a blanket at the edge of the city we watch the pale hemisphere shake off airplanes, blinking satellites, whirring insects fat as grapes, cloud ribbons writing code . . . we rouse together . . . breathe in as if floating . . . out as if flying . . . the slow tonal total hemisphere open . . . and distance . . .

AARON SHURIN'S books include the poetry collections *Involuntary Lyrics* (Omnidawn, 2005) and *The Paradise of Forms* (Talisman House, 1999), and, most recently, *King of Shadows*, a collection of personal essays, published by City Lights Books in 2008. His work has appeared in over thirty national and international anthologies, and has been translated into seven languages. Shurin's honors include writing fellowships from the National Endowment for the Arts, the California Arts Council, the San Francisco Arts Commission, and the Gerbode Foundation. He has lived in San Francisco since 1974, where he is a Professor in the MFA in Writing Program at the University of San Francisco.